AF405546

THE POSITIVE POETRY CLOSET

PRIYANKHA KAMALAKANNAN

FOREWORD

Dear Readers,

This poetry book is dedicated to the world, my inspiration. Each little thing around me forms a poem in my mind, and now I am sharing my collection with you. I want my poems to make you feel happy and loved because every human who is filled with positive energy can make this world a happy, loving place. After reading this, I hope you will be feeling positive, ready to make a big impact to the world. Share this energy-filled poetry book with everybody you know and bring all the happiness.

-Priyankha

LIFE
&
FUN

Lockdown

Doors closing, blinds down,

A child walking by with a sad frown.

Social distance, masks on,

All the people long gone.

Big parties all banned,

This is the government's command.

We all know that this wasn't planned,

A situation some cannot understand.

Creating economic distress,

Everybody struggling to progress.

Families conscious of health,

The true meaning of wealth.

The importance of love and joy,

We cannot destroy.

Humans losing control,

Complicated futures ready to unfold.

At a time like this, hand in hand,

We hope we withstand.

Let us not drown,

Together we will beat this LOCKDOWN.

True Friends

We stick together like glue,

We belong together like fries and burgers.

We have each other's backs,

We hold eternal trust.

We know each other inside out,

Sharing what we're all about.

Our friendship is too strong,

No one can prove us wrong.

Not even the hardest challenges.

But from all of this,

There is one thing I know,

That we are true friends.

Family Life

Loved ones you can trust,

Not people to ever mistrust.

You are a part of them,

They will never let you down.

Treat family like precious gems,

Because those people will never let you frown.

You might fight along the way,

But everything will become better the next day.

We share our Joy and share our sorrows,

But we come back together with more love tomorrow.

No matter whatever happens, we are always together,

Because you know that family is forever.

Imagine to Live

If you have no sense of imagination,

You'll have no humor.

If you have no humor,

You'll have no laughter.

If you have no laughter,

You'll have nothing to enjoy.

If you have nothing to enjoy,

You'll have no happiness.

If you have no happiness,

Then what's the point of life?

The Time I spilled my Yogurt

Oh! The time I spilled my Yogurt,

Was a moment I remember well,

Pale pink blobs all over my skirt,

Is a story I must tell.

You see, one day at recess,

I opened my lunch bag,

I started chanting the alphabet.

Hoping for a ticket to 6 flags.

But I saw that nothing was there,

Other than a round cup of Yogurt.

I thought that was not very fair,

So, I received some comfort.

Then I started eating my Yogurt,

As you are aware,

I scooped a big dollop,

And popped it in my mouth.

There I found a dollar,

Just lying there about.

I slowly went down to pick it up,

Forgetting that I had Yogurt in my hands.

I was about to pick the dollar,

Then I had realized what I had done,

It was that very moment that I saw the Yogurt on my skirt.

I opened my mouth to scream,

But no sound came out.

So, as people passed by,

They beamed with laughter about.

I was furious, so I ran to wipe the Yogurt,

I couldn't stand it anymore.

Oh, dear me! It was such a long time ago,

Now I just think of it as a funny scenario.

When the Chicken crossed the Road

Did you know what happens when chickens
cross the road?

No, it's not that the chickens get scared.

Because I am going to tell you the story of a
chicken who crossed the road.

It all began on a sunny summer day,

When a chicken walked astray.

The chicken walked for some time,

Around the bushes, collecting dimes.

And soon it reached a stage,

Where it needed to cross the road.

But instead of waiting for the cars to go,

The chicken flew over the cars!

And it flew on and on and on,

All around the globe!

When it landed back on that same road crossing,

It dizzily walked back to its home.

This is what happens to chickens,

Who are too lazy to wait to cross the road.

Don't be a chicken,

And watch out when crossing roads.

AMONG US
(Inspired by the game among us)

There were ten of us crammed around the table when we started,

One by one we all departed.

Everything seemed as normal as it could be,

Except for one thing: The impostor was still free.

I bumped into yellow on my way,

He looked quite suspicious on this very day.

A few seconds later, a body was reported,

All of us knew that suspicions would be recorded.

When we all came back to the table, there were only nine of us left,

Because the impostor has caused a terrible theft.

Lime said the body of purple was found

On the cold ground of electricals.

Immediately we all turned around,

And stared at Red,

Because he was the only one near the dead.

Each and every one of us accused him of treason,

We didn't let him give his reason.

Out and about did Red fly away,

But soon we found out that Red was safe.

The remaining eight again parted,

Even though we knew the impostor had darted.

We went to do our tasks,

Checking behind our backs.

Because the impostor is still AMONG US.

Humor

Humor is what you need,

To make people laugh.

Clowning around and telling jokes,

This is better than reading funny books.

Fake it, make it,

A thing to laugh about.

You need to know you are not funny,

Until someone's nose is runny.

Junky Food

Pizza, Pasta, Pepsi, Cola,

Mother recommends Granola.

Ketchup, Mayo, French fries,

They're messing with your eyes.

Cupcakes, Cookies, coffee, cake,

This reminds me, I need to take a break.

Lazy WKNDS

On a Saturday morning, we awaken to hear everyone snoring,
Some find this very boring.
A few hours gone by, and it's noon,
Sleepers feel like they are on the moon.
The rest of the day is spent lazing around,
Then mother comes home and says, "Get Out!".
So, we all trudge back to our favorite spots,
Making sure we don't get caught.
We try till dinner, then we race to the table,
When we grab our phones, the internet is disabled.
The big storm must have blown the connection,

This feels like a nasty infection.

We all moan around, and start to cry,

And when mom asks why,

We say "bye!".

Then we run up the stairs, and jump in our beds,

We were hoping for a better day instead.

Who knows what,

A better day always lies ahead!

NATURE
&
CREATURES

Nature

From green landscapes to leafy forests,

Or blossoming flowers and strange vines,

As well as the high mountains,

Which leads to the long rivers,

Or spiky shrubs and tall trees,

A wonderful sight to see,

Are the large tides of the sea.

But I have one question,

Have you ever thought about what nature is to you?

Well, I did and now I know,

The true meaning of this wonderful green world.

I now know that our nature protects us,

And we should protect them.

I now know that nature is everywhere,

And I now know what nature truly means to me.

Nature means peace.

Nature means positivity.

Nature means inspiration.

Nature means love.

Nature means that you are in a whole new world.

Nature is there to help you and guide you throughout life.

So, go ahead and give nature a little thanks.

The Five Elements

These are the five elements that created the earth.

These are the five elements that we humans thrive on.

Fire, blazing hot in deep shades of Red and Orange.

Water, crystal clean, as clear as can be.

Land, vast and broad, colorful, and interesting.

Air, the un-destroyable, invisible.

Sky, blue, cloudy, the mysterious.

The elements of life.

The elements of earth.

The elements, we are one with them.

A Green World

(An award-winning Poem in Pangolin contest - https://pangolin.green/creative-arts-inspiration/a-green-world-poem/)

A Green world is all we need,

To make our lives succeed.

It all starts from a single seed,

The right medicine for Mother Earth indeed.

Our dear, strong, Planet is slowly crumbling,

Soon we'll all be 'round and tumbling,

Going upon the ground that's stumbling,

Counting down the days that have been numbering.

Not every place is like Hawaii.

With blue, beautiful seas.

GMOs killing innocent bees,

Emptying the hives in the trees.

No more pollen,
The beauty of the world has fallen.
This should be a word of caution,
The Earth is now a devastating exhaustion.

Strange weather leading to animal extinction,
Destroying habitats in the distance.
Always a changing life condition,
Putting humanity in a difficult position.

Careless twigs, burning down the forests,
Lives of plants being demolished,
You know, to be honest,
Humanity cannot forfeit.

Leave the trees,
Just let them be,
Because there is no Planet B.

Anyhow, they're there to heal the planet, you see.

Spreading trees and plants around,
Will make the potential of this planet unbound.
We must make this message to sound,
Put a foot down on the ground.

Stop your car and ride your bike,
Or you can go on a hike.
You can see what we sustainable humans like,
We'll be joyful when a green civilization will strike.

Turn off the tap every time,
You can always save an extra dime.
We're looking for green in our lifetime,
Let's make healing Earth's wounds our pastime.

The new evolution,
Carrying over the pollution,
All over, even in the Ocean,
It's harm has been proven.

Littering and littering,
Although we know not to.
Causing pollution to stay there lingering,
Although it ought not to.

Reuse, reduce, recycle.
Every resource is vital,
Because there is no revival.
No revival, no survival,
This fact has no denial.

Limit the waste,
That's of good taste,
Because a wasteful world will be a disgrace.

This   fact   we   need   to   embrace.

Wisely use the paper,
And help save nature,
If not, we'll soon be living in a crater,
Hotter than the Equator.

Say no to plastic,
And make the environment enthusiastic.
Pollution is only drastic,
No, it's not fantastic.

Carbon dioxide, removing Oxygen,
We're trying to be approximate.
A big, terrible, consequence,
We can still survive with our confidence.

Towering over us is climate change,
It's time to make the greenhouse Gases arranged,
A dry, deserted Earth seems strange,
We all need to engage.

Earth is not our servant,
It is there and observant.
You should know that this is most urgent,
Because of the growing burden.

The protection and health of Mother Earth,
We all need to observe.
A better future we can unearth,
In the end we'll be thanked for our worth.

Working together as one team,
To conquer our dream.
Don't just daydream,
We must make the green regime supreme.

So many problems, but plenty solutions,

Let's put them into perfect execution.

Just turn around and take a think,

What more can we do to make our world

Green?

Trees

Trees and its leaves

Flying through the breeze

Its shaking with ease

The bees coming out their hive in the trees

Our trees guarantee lifelong peace

So please lets save our trees

The Beach

The beach is a fun place to be
Shells at the shore you can see
Sandcastles and surfing Oh! So much to see
Swimming and Snorkeling seeing lot of fish
Eating Ice cream is perfect for the beach
Enjoy the sunny weather at the cool,
refreshing beach

The Ocean

Big blue splashing waves,
The large underwater world,
Beautiful to see.

Lavender

Purple Lavender
Beautiful and relaxing
Soothing and vibrant

Daisies

A Dainty Daisy
It is a Pretty Flower
Small and tiny now

Birds

Cluck! Cluck! Cluck! Goes the rooster in the morning,
Duck! Duck! Duck! Say the children at the pond.
Quack! Quack! Quack! Are the duck's responses,
Crack! Crack! Crack! The eggs are going to hatch.
Chirp! Chirp! Chirp! The new babies are awake,
Slurp! Slurp! Slurp! Go the hungry little birds.
Flap! Flap! Flap! The birds are flying around,
Clap! Clap! Clap! Let's appreciate these cute creatures.

Animals

Animals, they can be big like an elephant,

Or small like a mouse.

Animals, they can be as fluffy as cats,

Or as rough as a crocodile's skin.

Animals, they can be as hard to find as chameleons,

Or they can be as easy to spot as a blue spotted frog.

Animals, they can be as fast as cheetahs,

Or they can be as slow as tortoises.

Animals, they can be what we humans can't,

But they can't be what we humans are.

Animals, they are unique,

Just like humans.

So dear reader, animals,

Their lives are as precious as our own.

We must work together, to save the animals.

For the animals, are there to save us.

Insects

From little creepy-crawlies to huge hornets,

This earth is home to many creatures.

Some deadly and some cute,

Some make sound like beautiful flutes.

Detailed and colorful,

Their creation is wonderful.

With the bees who make honey,

And help the flowers bloom,

And the wriggly tiny worms,

Who crawl through apples.

Oh, don't forget the long caterpillars,

Who turn into majestic butterflies.

Fascinating to see are the tiny ant camps,

Full of workers carrying large loads.

The world of insects is big and bright,

We welcome you to this exquisite realm.

SPACE
&
SEASONS

SUN

So very boiling hot
Upon the starry skies
None other is like our sun

MOON

Majestic moonlight from the Moon
Only a reflection from the Sun
Over the skies going around our home
Now a place full of mysteries

EARTH

In our earth there is day and night
As well as it is sunny and bright
The sun is producing all this light
Humanity creating deathly fights
No other beings in sight

STARS

Shining through the dark night
Twinkling so bright
And they bring a lot of light
Running around the universe
Sparkling stars they are

GALAXY

Gathering many stars of the night
Always available in different patterns
Like spiral or irregular, so much to know
As our Galaxy is called the Milky Way
eXpect the miracles they can bring
You and the world can explore today

Winter

On Icy winter days, you see snowflakes falling to the ground,
You can hear the wind howling, like a bloodhound.
You see a frosty layer of Ice, slippery like a slide,

You can see children and their toboggans, ready for a ride.

You hear laughter, from people in snowball fights,

Finishing the day's fun, before the cold nights.

When you walk into your home, you can smell a warm winter meal,

So deliciously warm, you can't believe it's real.

Before you go to bed, a warm cup of hot cocoa is there,

You walk over to the crackling fire and sit in a cozy chair.

Snowy days

Snowy days are one of those days

Where you wake up in the morning and open the window

Peeking over to see the white blanket of snow

So, you get ready fast, and you run down the stairs

And out into the garden to see the fluffy snow

And that feeling when you step into the snow

You feel the snow crunch beneath your soles

The satisfaction is endless

When you dig your hands into that thick layer

And you scoop a handful of snow

And throw it all the way across at someone else

Those snowball fights are always fun

When you end up with your toes numb,
fingers frozen and cheeks rosy red
All you want is a nice cup of warm hot
chocolate
 The warm mug is what always soothes you
after a long snowy day

Snowflakes

Unique little flakes
Of Cold, Icy and Frosted snow
Microscopic shapes

SPRING

So lovely spring

Pretty plants you bring

Rain dances when you sing

I don't know what your colorful rainbows will think

Now is the time for the bright light that shines

Gazing at the meadows spring brings

Summer

Sunny, warm days
Under the shining rays
From winter to now, a lot of weather change
Let's enjoy the last of these beautiful days
This time we can be swimming, singing and partying
All in the beautiful time of summer

Autumn

Falling leaves during autumn
Red, Orange, Yellow, Brown
So many different colored leaves
Let's make a leaf pile
That touches the high sky
Here comes a Pumpkin harvest
With lots of other fun times

Rainy days

It first starts with a little drizzle,

Rain drops you can barely hear,

Soon comes down the pouring rain,

Bashing against the windows.

Tiny little raindrops,

Falling from high, wet, clouds.

Umbrellas shielding you from a downpour of rain,

But the heavy wind takes control,

And soon it flies away.

As you walk on the streets,

You can feel the wetness of the rain on your skin.

Your hair soon turns into a pile of wet strands.

When you reach home,

You dry off and become warm,

And you realize that is always something good,
On windy, rainy days.

Clouds

Clouds, clouds floating in the air

You come in different shapes

You can be part of a landscape

Sometimes it's fun to find out your shape

You may be a unicorn or a comb

Or a dragon and a drone

Sometimes we imagine of floating on a cloud and

Riding it down a rainbow

But we know all of this is just our imaginative brains

OCCASIONS & LOCATIONS

Diwali

Shining lights floating around,
You can hear the firecracker sound.
This religious festival we all enjoy,
I will tell you why if you will stand hereby.
In the north they say,
That on this auspicious day,
Ram, Sita and Lakshman, returned to their kingdom Ayodhya after 14 years.
In the south it is believed,
God Krishna defeated the demon Narakasura,
On this occasional day.
Even though the interpretations are not the same,
Now you can see, what this day became.
On the day of the festival of lights, Diwali or Deepavali,
We are all connected through light.

Christmas

Christmas is a jolly time
To laugh and play with family
Every Sunday light a candle
Until the 4th Sunday
Christmas Eve is time for a big dinner
With stuffed Turkey and apple pie
Also, leave some cookies and carrots
For Santa and his reindeers
Next morning we all wake up to many presents
Prancing with Joy

HAPPY NEW YEAR

Now the year comes to an end

Every time we start again

We celebrate the New Year with firecrackers and more

You and I have bright future ahead

Either going smooth or hectic

Above it all we must enjoy

Remembering each and every beginning of the year

Halloween

Halloween is the harvesting time
Nowadays you spooked out by the decorations
Dressing up in scary, crazy costumes
Everyone decorating and passing out candy
Halloween is the spookiest time of the year

EASTER

Easter eggs are to be found
At the time of Easter
So enjoy finding all the eggs
Then also to find the Easter bunny
Every year we shall not forget
Running to find the eggs

ANCIENT ROME

Oh Ancient Rome, was a big place

Taking over northwestern Europe to the near east

Eating bread dipped in fine wine

Tunic and sandals is what they mainly wore

The government was not fair when making the laws

That is how life was in ancient Rome

ANCIENT EGYPT

The Egyptian of the Ancient times

Were fascinating to know about

Pyramids and Tombs old and rusty

All made by the smart minds of the Egyptians

Cleopatra, Tutankhamun and Hatshepsut

All people known by the Egyptians

Cultural life of the Egyptians is the
foundation of our own

SPORT & SKILLS

Cricket

Cricket, It's all about the wickets,

On a green lengthy pitch.

With bat and ball,

It's a great game after all.

Six or none,

Each ball is always fun.

With bets and bids,

To find those who are highly skilled,

At the wonderful game of cricket.

Play the game with the right spirit,

Then you'll feel like you've hit it.

Badminton

Over the net, there flies so fast

It's the shuttle or the badminton ball.

Alongside is the badminton racket,

Which is quite long,

But it is very strong.

Game so fast, you can't keep track,

But make sure it doesn't hit your back.

Make your way to twenty-one

Then you will know you've won.

Way to GOAL!

Here comes the pass,

The ball goes fast.

The goalie is steady,

But I am more than ready.

1,2,3 KICK!!!

All I need is a little flick.

The ball flies up and above,

It scared away a Dove.

This is a save, the goalie cannot make,

This is an opportunity I will take.

I let the ball come back down,

And give the opponents a frown,

Because... I kick the ball and score a

GOOAAL!!

Movies

These man-made moving picture

Can be seen at home or the cinema

With popcorn and more treats

There are different types of movies

Movies for kids, movies for adults

Also in different languages

Movies can be watched anytime anywhere

With family or alone

Dancing

Some people think dancing is when

You move gracefully across the stage

Others think different

The skill and time it takes

To be able to master the art of your own

dance

There are so many types of dancing

Popular ones are Ballet, Hip Hop or

Breakdance

But you have your own style

You choose how you move

Move the way you want.

Art

A talent that can be showed in many different
ways
Raging with passion from artists
This masterpiece is unique in its own way

Books

Biographies, Mysteries and non-fiction, so
much to choose from
On shelves, more, and everywhere
Overtaking your daydreams
Kids and Adults, reading makes you strong
So read and learn some more

School

School is to educate us

Creating knowledgeable minds

Here we also have lots of fun

Our fun is in the learning

Our school is a place where we all feel welcome

Lovely teachers, friends and more

Music

When you see the birds,

They are singing.

You can hear their words,

The branches of trees are swinging.

Listen to a song,

The tunes are ringing.

This is the thing,

The Instruments are bringing.

When we are happy,

The energetic music comes.

When we are sad,

The music become the energetic one.

At night, when you go to bed,

You want a sweet melody playing.

All of this said,

This is what music is saying.

COLORS

White

Color of fluffy clouds,

Huddling together in crowds.

Color of thin Paper,

Coming from great nature.

Color of soft snow,

Before its texture will go.

Color of cute polar bears,

With fuzzy hair.

Color of plain milk,

Flowing perfectly like silk.

Color of most of our world,

The color that makes more colors.

That color is WHITE.

Blue

There are many things on our planet,

And they are as blue as can be.

Like oceans with tall, blue waves.

Or like ripped, baggy jeans.

There is so much blue to see,

So, look around carefully.

You can see sourly sweet blueberries,

Resting on bushes.

Or little raindrops falling to the ground.

The skies with the range of blues,

Navy inks slathered on paper,

And huge whales leaping over the water.

Here and there and everywhere,

This BLUE can be anywhere.

Yellow

Bright yellow bananas,

The blazing yellow sun.

Citric yellow lemons,

A large yellow leaf.

Tall yellow sun flowers,

Round yellow egg yolks.

Squishy yellow sponge,

Delicious yellow cheese.

Small yellow taxis,

Cute yellow chicks.

There are many things that you can see,

That are as YELLOW as can be.

Red

Fiery, bloody red,

Fierce fire, with strong flames.

Dark blood, dripping from a finger.

Shiny apples, sour and sweet.

Aromatic roses, with a smell so powerful.

Spicy chilies, which burns your tongue.

Small strawberries, a delicacy.

Juicy watermelons, a colorful surprise.

Fluttering ladybugs spotted and delicate.

Autumn leaves, slowly dropping to the floor.

Our earth, endlessly RED.

FOOD

Fruits

Juicy, healthy, delicious fruits,

Amazing varieties nature has brought to you.

From all over the world, at least you must have had one,

But most people have eaten a ton.

They are uncountable,

It cannot possibly be done,

Unless you spend your whole life,

Counting the uncountable.

You have apples, bananas, oranges, and mangoes,

Or grapes, blueberries, strawberries and raspberries.

This is just one hundredth of all the fruits we know,

The more you travel, the more you will discover.

Sour fruits, sweet fruits, tasteless fruits and juicy fruits.

So many ways to describes the taste of fruits exist,

It's up to you to create many more.

But have you ever imagined,

Where all these fruits came from?

Some come from trees,

Some come from bushes,

Some even come from vines.

But you won't find everything everywhere,

Bananas grow only when it's hot,

Try not to imagine, bananas in the snow.

Apples only grow when it's windy and cold,

Don't even think of seeing them on a beach,

Hanging out with palm trees.

But have you even realized the values of these fruits?

Not only the taste or it's smell,

Most of the time people eat them to stay healthy.

Fruits give you energy,

Fruits give you vitamins,

Fruits make you full,

You could even survive on a diet of just fruits!

Dear people, now I hope you know the value,

Of our endless fruits.

We must help them grow,

We must help them live,

We must keep them safe,

They don't care about allies and enemies,

They are there for all.

So, let's be there for them every day,

Because they will always be there for us.

Vegetables

They help you stay healthy for lifetime
Also gives strength and energy
For this helps you to survive
Many different kinds and colors
Mushroom, carrots let your taste choose
Tomato, broccoli, healthy it shall be
For vegetables are as healthy as they can be

Pizza

Pizza mamma mia
Cheese and tomatoes
Unique but beautiful
Juicy and scrumptious
What a delicacy

Sweets

Sweets, sweets of different shape, form & taste
Jellybeans and gummy bears, colorful beauty
Sugary chocolate out of factories
All this candy is sure tasty
But it's not healthy
Have a balance of sweet and healthy

Spices

Rosemary, Oregano, Basilikum and Thyme
Flavors food very fine
Makes food a lot better than it is
It'll be delicious and ready in a whiz!

ABOUT THE AUTHOR

 Priyankha Kamalakannan is a keen reader, writer, and creative thinker living in Germany. Her passion for literature is what brought her to write books. Priyankha likes to devote a lot of time and effort whenever it comes to writing or reading. She also connects a lot of her life to writing, such as her Ted talk, her website, her YouTube channel, and participation in external events. However, she mostly loves spending time with friends and family.

Email: priyankha.itsme@gmail.com
Fantasia Adventures – Priyankha Kamalakannan (available on Amazon)
Ted Talk:The Power of Writing | Priyankha Kamalakannan | TEDxYouth@TFIS
Website: http://www.priyankhakamal.com/
YouTube Channel: Priyankha K

79